Time for PHONICS

2

Marion Ireland

COMBINING
PHONETIC SOUNDS

HUNTER
EDUCATION
NIGHTINGALE

Copyright © 2018 Marion Ireland
Time for Phonics Book 2

Published by:
Hunter Education Nightingale
ABN: 69 055 798 626
PO Box 547
Warners Bay NSW 2282
Ph: 0417 658 777
email: sales@huntereducationnightingale.com.au
        paul@huntereducationnightingale.com.au
        www.huntereducationnightingale.com.au

Cover Design: Brooke Lewis

National Library of Australia Card No.
and ISBN 978 - 1 - 925787 - 05 - 4
Phonics Series ISBN 978 - 1 - 925787 - 08 - 5

RECYCLING

When the program is completed and the paper no longer wanted, be sure to have it recycled.
The time and care taken to recycle may help save a tree and maintain our environment.

E	D	C	B	A
22	21	20	19	18

About this Book - *and how to get the best out of it.*

- **Pre Test** single sounds. Revise as needed.

- **Directions** in smaller print need to be read aloud to students to give them a clear understanding of what they need to do.

- **A phonic approach** using oral phonemic awareness strategies (80% of words in the English language have a phonic base)

- **Word families** consisting of many simple rhyming words. This base list can be expanded as relevant.

- **Varied, graded activities** that are age appropriate.

- **Core words** - simple common sight words that are also high frequency words essential to all reading matter.

- **Challenge activities** are incorporated in the mix.

- **Personal Word Box** - words chosen by student and/or teacher, based on student needs. These need to be achievable for individual students.

- **Blends** - are included as they form an essential part of many word families.

- **Graded sentences** can form the basis of Dictation and show correct usage of list words. These can be modified as needed.

- **Sentence construction** - students are encouraged to complete and create some of their own oral and written sentences.

- **Compound words** - an introduction to compound words using known words selected from word families.

- **Revision** is built into the sequence of activities.

- **Assessment tasks** measure progress and can also be used as a diagnostic tool.

Message to Parents

With *Time for Phonics Book 2* you may need and want to help your child with some of the word families introduced to make more complex words. As a parent you can work with your child to ensure the basic fundamentals of learning to read with Phonics. Follow the suggested approach with each sound, blend and sentence and as your child's understanding and competence grows reading skills will grow too.

As your child works through the book your help may be required less. However, ensure your child fully understands the process and outcomes of a phonetic approach to reading. Good spelling and writing will follow.

Praise your child at all times, because you are the ideal support person in your child's life to help with developing a good education. It is essential that your child learns to read. *Time for Phonics 2* will provide a brick in the foundations of learning to read. Work with your child, make the learning process fun and enjoy the journey to becoming a good reader.

Run the sounds *a* and *n* together to form *an*.

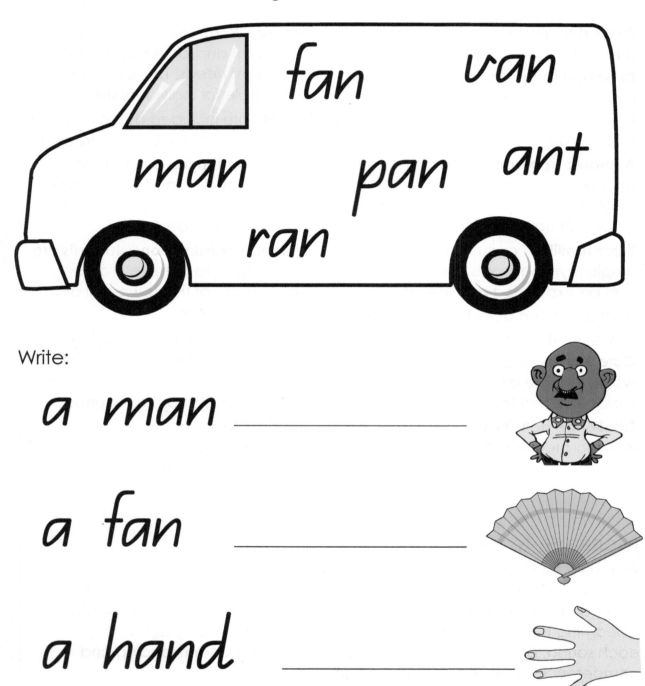

fan van

man pan ant

ran

Write:

a man _____

a fan _____

a hand _____

Run the sounds *i* and other letters together and say them aloud.
Read and write them.

in   is   it   if

____   ____   ____   ____

Write **an** in these words. Run the sounds together to read and spell each word aloud.

m____   p____   ____d

v____   f____   h____d

      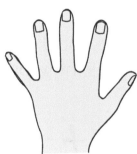

Read and spell.

A man ran.

Dan is in a van.

An ant ran in a pan.

My Word Box

Run the sounds *a* and *t* together to form *at*.

bat   fat   pat

mat   cat   hat   sat   rat

Add the middle sound *a*, then run the sounds together to read and spell the words. Write each word on the line.

f__t _____

s__t _____

p__t _____

c__t _____

to and *do* are sight words.

my and *by* have a long *i* sound for letter *y*.

to   do   my   by

_____   _____

Write these words.

a bat _____

my hat _____

the rat _____

Read and spell.

A fat cat ran.

I sat by my hat in the van.

That man can pat my fat rat.

My Word Box

Run the *a* and *d* sounds together to form *ad*.

Read and spell the *ad* words and write them on the *ladder*.

dad   had

mad   pad

sad   bad

lad   add

no, *go* and *so* each begin with a short sound but the *o* has a long sound.

no   go   so   as

_____   _____   _____   _____

Write the middle sounds.

The m_n in

the h_t is

my d_d.

Read and spell.

Dad can go to the van.

Dad is mad at the bad rat.

This bad lad is sad. He is mad.

My Word Box

Special Blends

Practise making the sounds *th* sounds, then copy the *th* words.

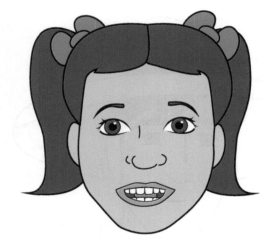

the _____

this _____

that _____   than _____

mother _____

father _____

My Word Box

Practise making the *sh* sounds, then copy the *sh* words.

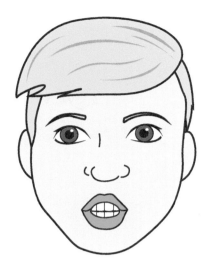

she _____

shed _____

shop _____ shin _____

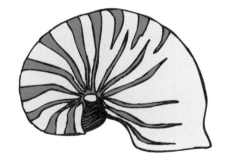

a _ __ell

a ___ip

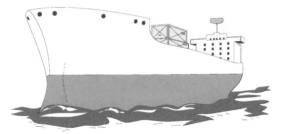

My Word Box

Run the sounds *a* and *p* together to form *ap*.

Add *p* to finish these words. Run the sounds together to read and spell *ap* words aloud. Copy each word.

ta__ _____ la__ _____

ca__ _____ na__ _____

ma__ _____ ra__ _____

sa__ _____ sla__ _____

cla__ _____ tra__ _____

Run the sounds together aloud. Read and write them.

on   mum   did   big

____ _____ _____ _____

Label the pictures with *ap* words.

Read and spell.

Go to my big tap.

I can clap my hands.

My big cap is on my lap.

My Word Box

Run the sounds **a** and **m** together to form **am**. Add **m** to finish these words. Run the sounds together to read and spell the words aloud.

Pa__   Sa__   da__   ha__

ja__   ra__   tra__   pra__

Write **am** to finish these words.

S___ is in a pr___.

P___ is a mum.

A r___ is at the d___.

e has a long sound in these words. Copy them neatly.

me   he   we   be

_____   _____   _____   _____

Draw:

a tin of jam

a ram

This is me on a big tram.

Read and spell.

Pam and Sam had jam.

My ram is at the dam. He is big.

Pam did go home in a tram.

She is a mum.

My Word Box

Run the sounds *a* and *g* together to form *ag*.

Read and spell these words aloud. Copy each word.

bag _____   wag _____

sag _____   rag _____

flag _____   tag _____

ee has a long *e* sound in **bee** and **see**. *e* has a **short** sound in **yes**.
put is a sight word.

bee   see   yes   put

_____

Put a bee on my hat.

Put a flag on this bag.

Read and spell:

He can see a bee on my bag.

We can see a tag on my bag.

Yes. She put a flag on that bag.

My Word Box

Run the sounds *e* and *t* together to form *et*. Write the missing vowel sounds in the *et* word family. Run the sounds together to read and spell these words aloud.

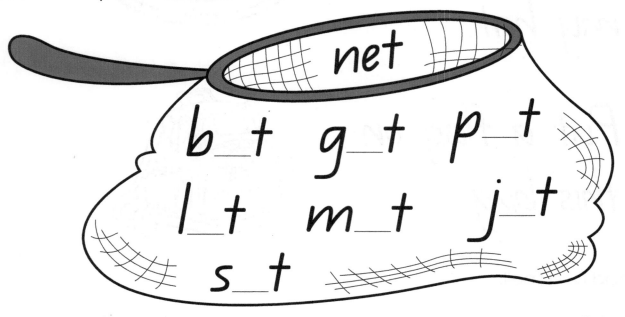

net

b_t   g_t   p_t

l_t   m_t   j_t

s_t

Label these pictures.

   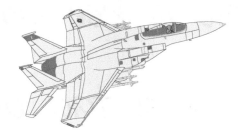   

_____   _____   _____

Use phonic clues to read *baby* and *little*.

one and *two* are sight words.

baby   little   one   two

_____   _____   _____

Finish this sentence about a **jet**.

A jet can _____

_____

Join the words to match each picture.

my big jet   a little baby   two pets

Read and spell:

My pet cat is wet.

See my big jet go up.

The little baby is one. She can

get two pets.

My Word Box

Run the sounds *e* and *d* together to form *ed*. Write the missing vowel sounds in the *ed* word family. Read and spell these words aloud.

bed   r_d   l_d

T_d   t_ddy

f_d   sh_d

Write the missing sounds to match each picture.

my __ed    my __eddy

a __ed cap   a ___ed

Run the sounds together aloud. Read and write these words.

his   has   have   shed

_____ _____ _____ _____

Put a tick next to the sentence that matches the picture.

I sat on a big bed.

I fed my red teddy.

I fed my cat.

Read and spell.

Ted fed his pet cat.
I have a teddy. It is red.
Fred put it on my bed in
the shed.

My Word Box

Run the sounds *e* and *n* together to form *en*. Write the missing vowel sounds in the *en* word family. Run the sounds together to read and spell these words aloud.

hen   p__n   d__n   t__n   m__n

B__n   th__n   w__nt   wh__n

Run the sounds together to read and spell the *en* words aloud and finish these:

m___ _____

h___ _____

10 t___ _____

Run the sounds together aloud. Read and write these words.

him   its   up   but

_____   _____   _____   _____

Finish this sentence about a **hen**.

My little red hen can _____

_____

Draw:

a little red hen	ten pens

Read and spell:

Ben has a pet hen.

Ten men ran from the den.

Ben went to put his hen in

a pen when dad let him.

My Word Box

Run the sounds together for *eg* and *ep* words. Write them neatly. Read and spell them aloud.

be___   le___   pe___   eg___   Me___

Write the labels for these pictures.

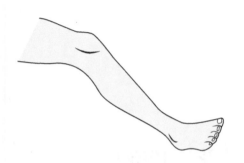  

___ ___ ___ ___   ___ ___ ___ ___   ___ ___ ___

pep
step

___ ___ ___

___ ___ ___ ___

Use sounds to help you read and spell these.

got   not   down   play

___ ___ ___   ___ ___ ___   ___ ___ ___

Draw two pegs.

Draw two legs.

Write *eg* or *ep* in the spaces.

M____ has an ____g on her l___. She sat on the st___.

Read and spell:

My pet can beg a lot.
He sat down on the step and got wet.
We have got two legs that go up and down when we play.

My Word Box

25

Blends

cl fl gl pl sl

Practise making these sounds aloud. Run the sounds together. Where does your tongue go when you make these sounds? Copy words with these blends from your word families.

clap   _____

slam   _____

flag   _____

blog   _____

glad   _____

play   _____

fr pr tr dr gr

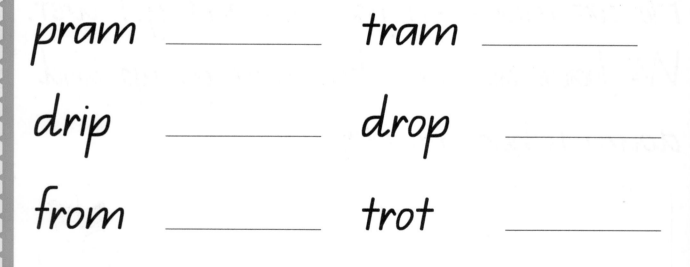

Slide these sounds together aloud to make these blends from your word families. Write each word neatly.

pram   _____

tram   _____

drip   _____

drop   _____

from   _____

trot   _____

grip   _____

grub   _____

sk st sp

Practise making these sounds aloud. Slide these sounds aloud to make these blends from your word families. Write each word neatly.

skip _____   skin _____

sky _____   skit _____

stag _____   stop _____

spin _____   spot _____

Label these pictures.

      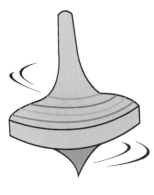

___ ___ ___ ___   ___ ___ ___ ___   ___ ___ ___ ___

My Word Box

Special Blends

Put your hand in front of your mouth when you make this sound.

What can you feel?

wh

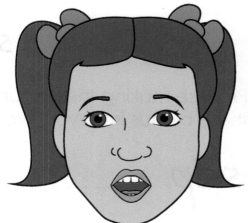

Sound these words using the *wh* sound.
Read and spell these words aloud. Copy them neatly.

when _____   *why* _____

Write *wh* in these words to match the pictures. Copy each word.

____ip      _____

____ale      _____

____eel   _____

____ite      _____

28

ch

chicken

chap   chip

chess

chop

Write *ch* in these words to match the pictures.

Sound these words using the *ch* sound.

Copy them neatly.

_____ip   _____

_____in   _____

_____ap   _____

_____op   _____

_____icken   _____

29

Double Consonants

Add *mm*. Read and copy this word.

tu____y _____

Add *tt*. Read and copy this word.

le____er _____

Add *dd*. Read and copy this word.

mi____le _____

Add *bb*. Read and copy this word.

bu____le _____

Some words join together to make one word called a compound word.

in + to = _____

kit + ten = _____

pig + let = _____

Assessment Task

Put a tick next to the words that match the picture.

a fat rat

a fat cat

a bad rat

a red flag

a big bag

a blue flag

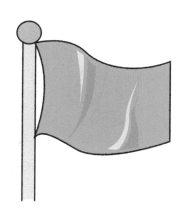

a baby in a pram

a baby in a tram

a ram in a pram

a hen in a shed

a hen in bed

a hen in a nest

Write the missing sounds.

__ap

ba__

__gg

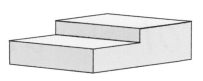

____ep

Run the sounds *i* and *g* together to form *ig*. Write the missing end sound in these *ig* words. Run the sounds together to read and spell these words aloud.

pig

di__

bi__

ri__

di__ piglet

wi__

fi__

Write *ig* in these words and read the sentence aloud..

This is my b____ mother

p____ and a little p____let.

f has a *v* sound in *of*. Now sound *off* with the *f* sound. *into* is two little words. *put* is a sight word but you can make the first and the last sounds. Copy each word.

of   off   into   put

____   ____   ____   ____

Do pigs beg? _____

Do pigs nap? _____

Do pigs get wet? _____

Do pigs play? _____

Read and spell:

A big fat pig ran to me.

He ran off into a dam and sat down.

See that little piglet. He can dig.

My Word Box

Run the sounds *i* and *n* together to form *in*. Write the missing end sounds in these *in* words. Run the sounds together to read and spell these words aloud.

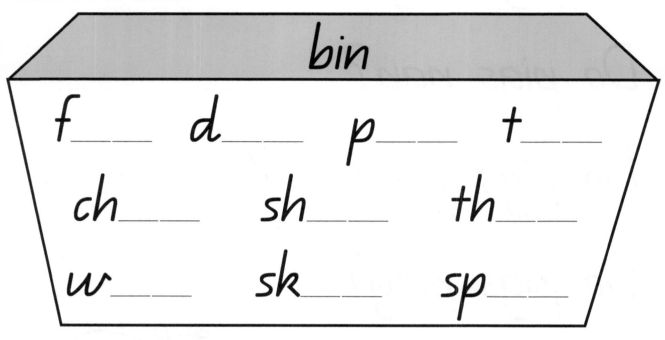

bin

f____ d____ p____ t____

ch____ sh____ th____

w____ sk____ sp____

Put a tick next to the sentence that matches the picture.

I sat on a pig.

I sat on a pin.

I sat on a tin.

Practise making the blends in these words.

y has an *i* sound at the end.

try   cry   fry   why

_____ _____ _____ _____

Copy these words and add **S** to make them more than one.

bin _____   fin _____

pin _____   tin _____

shin _____   chin _____

Read and spell:

I try to win. I sat on a pin.
The jam is in a little tin.
Why did dad put my tin in the
pig pen? I have to go and get it.

My Word Box

Combining Sounds - ip

Run the sounds *i* and *p* together to form *ip*. Write the missing *i* or *p* sounds in these words. Run the sounds together to read and spell these words aloud.

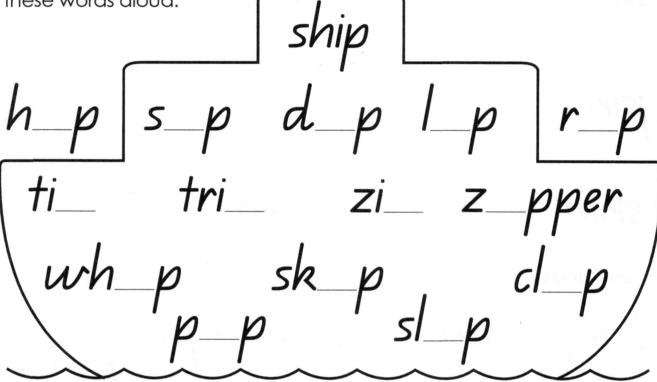

ship

h_p s_p d_p l_p r_p

ti__ tri__ zi__ z_pper

wh_p sk_p cl_p

p_p sl_p

Label these pictures.

_____   _____   _____

These are sight words but you can use phonic clues. *oy* makes a special sound.

boy   boys   toy   toys

_____   _____   _____

Write *ip* in these words and read the sentences aloud.

Sk_____ to mum and dad.

He put his toy sh_____ on his bed.

She went on a big tr_____.

I have two l_____s.

This is a z_____per.

Read and spell:

I can skip and go on a big trip.
His toy ship is red. Skip to me.
Ted put his whip on a toy ship
and went off to the boys.

My Word Box

Run the sounds *i* and *t* together to form *it*. Write *it* in these words.
Run the sounds together to read and spell these words aloud.

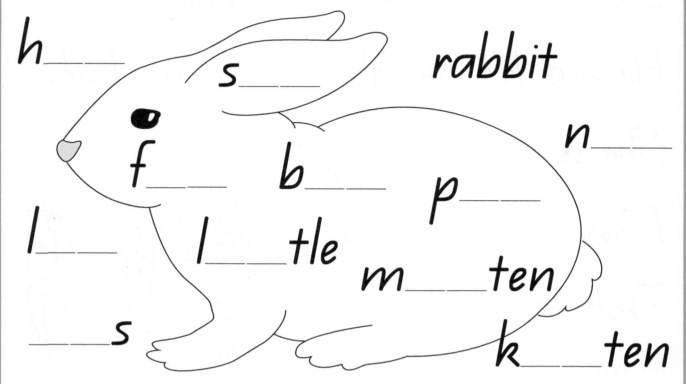

h____

s____

rabbit

n___

f___

b___

p___

l___

l___tle

m___ten

k___ten

____s

Write the missing words to match a picture.

Jim has a pet

_____.

His kitten is _____.

girl   girls   old   school

_____ _____ _____

Can boys and girls play? _____

Can I fly my bus in the sky? _____

Can we put a hat on a kitten? _____

Read and spell:

A kitten can sit on my lap.

As I got up my old rabbit

ran to a little girl.

The girls have two pet

rabbits and a little kitten at school.

My Word Box

Run the sounds *i* and **x** together to form *ix*. Write *ix* in these words and copy each one to match the picture.

6   s_____   _____

m_____   _____

f_____   _____

Look at **oo**. What sound does it make?   *or, for* and *four* are sight words.

too   or   for   four

_____   _____   _____   _____

Run the sounds *i* and *d* together to form *id*. Write *id* in these words and copy each one.

d_____   _____   h_____   _____

l____   _____   b____   _____

Write the missing letters to match each picture.

s_____ caps

The l_____ is on the jam.

Read and spell:

Mum did mix the jam for me.
Six boys and girls did go to school.
Four girls did go home to fix an old
bed that is too big for me.

Run the sounds *o* and *g* together to form *og*. Write *og* in these words. Run sounds together to read and spell them aloud.

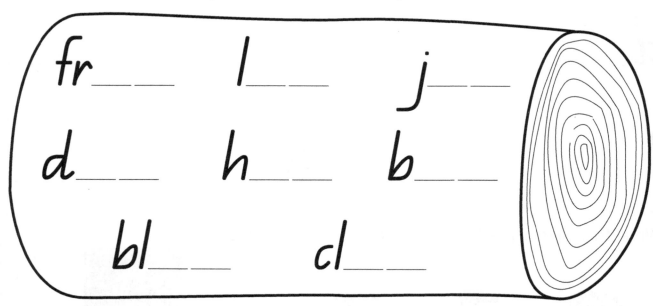

fr____   l____   j____

d____   h____   b____

bl____   cl____

Write the missing letters to match each picture.

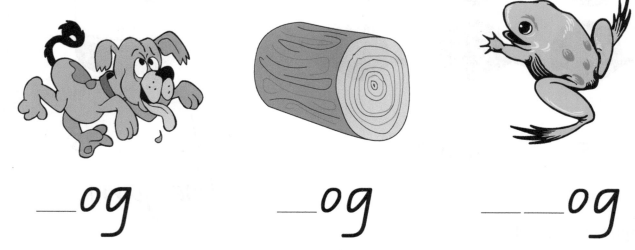

___og   ___og   ___og

Do you remember the sound that *th* makes? Sound out *jump*. *over* is a sight word.

this   that   jump   over

_____ _____ _____ _____

Read the sentences. Put a tick next to the one that matches the picture.

This is an old dog. He is wet.

This is an old hen on a nest.

This is a fat green frog on a log.

Boys and girls can jog at school.

Boys and girls can jump over the school.

Boys and girls can jog up a ladder.

We can go for a jog in the fog.

An old dog sat down on this log.

Why did two fat frogs jump over that wet bog?

My Word Box

Combining Sounds - on

Run the sounds **o** and **n** together to form **on**. Write **on** in these words and copy. Run sounds together to read and spell them aloud.

a b____b____   a p____d   a cray____

Combining Sounds - ox

Run the sounds **o** and **x** together to form **ox**. Write **ox** in these words and copy. Run sounds together to read and spell them aloud.

 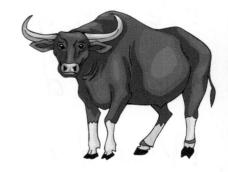

a b____   a f____   an ____

Make the **th** sound in these words. What sound does **ee** make in **three**.

then   them   with   three

_____ _____ _____ _____

How many bonbons? _____

How many boxes? _____

How many foxes?_____

How many crayons?_____

Read and spell:

Don can see a big red fox.
Do not let that bad fox
get his three hens.
Ron has six bonbons. He put three
of them in a box with a lid.

My Word Box

Run the sounds **o** and **p** together to form **op**. Write **op** to make rhyming words. Run sounds together and read them aloud.

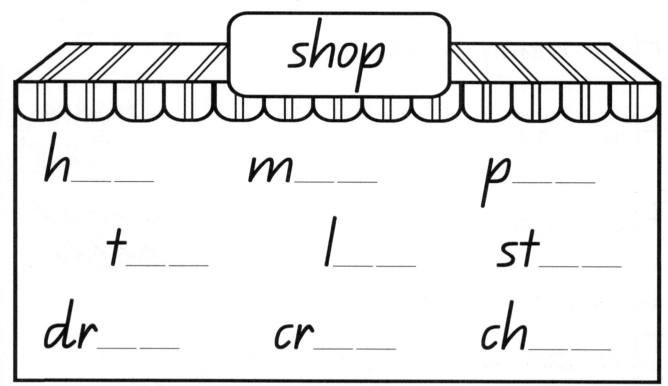

shop

h____   m____   p____

t____   l____   st____

dr____   cr____   ch____

Draw a line to match words to pictures.

a pet shop

a rusty old shed

Sound these words out aloud. What sound does **y** make at the end of *happy*?

just   must   rust   happy

_____

Write the missing *op* words to match the pictures.

The car must _____.

You can _____ on one leg.

I can go to the _____
to get a m_____.

Can you hop on top for me?
You must not play in the pet shop.
Just go home with Pop and get a
mop from the rusty old shed.

My Word Box

Run the sounds **o** and **t** together to form **ot**. Write the missing sounds. Run the sounds together to read and spell aloud.

 __ot

 __ot

 __ot

 __ot

 S__ot has spots.

My pony can ____ot.

Practise reading and spelling these sight words.

she   her   you   your

_____   _____   _____

Join the rhyming words in these boxes. Use a different colour for each different set of rhyming words.

box	not
got	fox
ox	lot

trot	top
hop	spot
pot	pop

Spot is a dog. That pot is hot.
Can you put baby and a lot
of toys in the cot?
You can play with her at home
when she is happy in her cot.

My Word Box

Run the sounds u and b together to form ub. Write the missing vowels and copy each word. Run the sounds together.

c__b _____   gr__b _____

r__b _____   cl__b _____

Do you know this nursery rhyme?

R__b a d__b d__b

Three men in a t__b

Write the missing words to match the pictures.

seven fox _____

five fat _____

Use phonic clues for these words. Copy each one.

four   five   six   seven

_____ _____ _____ _____

Circle the *ub* words in this box.

rub   cub   bud   grubs   home

bubble   rubble   tumble   club

dub   bub   cubby   tub   cubs

hub   hut   pub   subway   rubber

Read and spell:

One little grub is hot.
Do you have six or seven cubs?
Did you see that? I can see four
grubs in your cubby at school.

My Word Box

Run the sounds u and n together to form un. Write these words to match the pictures below.

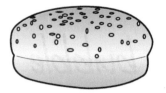

bun   sun   run

_____   _____   _____

Circle the word *fun* in *funny*.

Circle the word *bun* in *bunny*.

Circle the word *sun* in *sunny*.

Circle the word *run* in *runny*.

Sound the blends in *sky* and *fly*. Sound *can* + *not*. Use phonic clues for *home*.

sky   fly   cannot   home

_____   _____   _____

Yes or no?

Can a jet fly in the sky? _____

Can a bunny fly in the sky? _____

Can a frog fly in the sky?_____

Can pigs fly? _____

Read and spell:

It is fun to run in the sun.

Go and get a bun from the shop.

It is for mum.

A funny little bunny ran under
the red bus and over the top.

He cannot fly in the sky.

My Word Box

Combining Sounds - up

Run the sounds *u* and *p* together to form *up*. Write *up* in these words to match the pictures. Run the sounds together.

a c _ _ p   a p _ _ p

Combining Sounds - um

Run the sounds *u* and *m* together to form *um*. Write *um* in these words to match pictures. Run the sounds together.

dr _ _ _   pl _ _ _

Use phonic clues. *i* has a long sound in *like bike* and *hike*.

like   bike   hike   read

Circle the rhyming words in each row.

hum   mum   tub   sum

hen   up   cup   pup

gum   drum   plum   dam

Read and spell:

My pup sat down on a drum.
Mum put this toy pup on its
bike down by the cubby.
I like to go on a hike. When it is
too hot I read with mum and dad.

My Word Box

Combining Sounds - ud

Run the sounds *u* and *d* together to form *ud*.

bud   mud   spud   suds

Sound these words aloud. Write words to label these pictures.

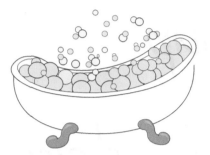  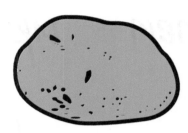

_____   _____   _____

These *ud* words all have *dd* in the middle. Put the words back together.

mu+dd+y = _____

pu+dd+le = _____

cu+dd+le = _____

Sound these words aloud. Read and spell them. Copy each one neatly.

next   text   help   left

_____   _____   _____

Circle 3 words that rhyme with *puddle*.

cuddle   rabbit   middle

huddle   ladder

little   muddy   muddle

Read and spell:

Do not sit in the mud.
Put the buds next to the
spuds on the box.
One wet day I went in a
very muddy puddle as I
went home from the book shop.

My Word Box

Run the sounds **u** and **g** together to form **ug**. Write **ug** to complete these words. Run the sounds together to read and spell them aloud.

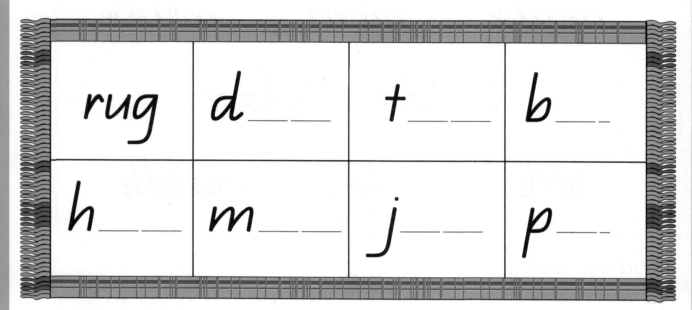

rug	d____	t____	b__
h____	m____	j__	p__

Draw a red jug

next to a mug

on a rug.

Use phonic clues to read and spell these words aloud. **er** on the end of these words has its own special sound. **a** has a different sound in **after**. It is a sight word.

ever   never   clever   after

_____   _____   _____   _____

Write a sentence using the word *hug*.

_____

_____

Read and spell:

A big fat bug sat down in the mud.
Put the red jug next to that hot
mug after I sit down.

Never put a mug and a jug on this
muddy rug. That is not clever.

My Word Box

Combining Sounds - us

Run the sounds **U** and **S** together to form **US**. Write the missing vowel sounds.

Look at __s.

W__ are in a

b__g r__d b__s.

Combining Sounds - ut

Run the sounds **U** and **t** together to form **ut**. Write **ut** in these words then copy them neatly.

c____   b____   h____   n____

Does **put** rhyme with **but**? _____

Practise **oo** in look and book. Use phonic clues for **open**.
our is a sight word.

look   book   open   our

_____   _____   _____   _____

Yes or no?

Can you go on a bus? _____

Can a bus cry? _____

Can a bus fly? _____

Can you cut a bun? _____

Can you shut a book? _____

Read and spell:

Look at this big red bus at the hut.
A girl and her dog are in our hut.
They left her in a bus.
Put our toy bus in the box then help
me shut the hut that she left open.

My Word Box

Assessment Task

PART 1

Colour the circle next to the word that does **not** rhyme.

Write words to match the pictures.

○ and
○ ant
○ hand

_____ _____

○ fox
○ dog
○ blog

_____ _____

○ mum
○ hum
○ pram

_____ _____

○ jet
○ wet
○ web

_____ _____

○ pin
○ ship
○ shin

_____ _____

Mark

$\overline{10}$

Mark   / 10

Assessment Task

Teacher direction: Say each word once. Read the sentence. Repeat the word.

PART 2

man	A man is a boy who has grown up.
sat	I sat on a chair.
had	We had our lunch outside.
tap	Water comes out of a tap.
jam	Do you like jam on toast?
wag	My dog can wag his tail.
pet	I have a pet bird.
bed	I sleep in a bed.
ten	I can count to ten.
leg	I hurt my leg when I fell over.
dig	I dig in the sand with my spade.
bin	Put your rubbish in the bin.
ship	A ship sails on the sea.
six	Six comes after five.
hid	The children hid under the table.

Mark /15

PART 3

kitten	A kitten is a baby cat.
put	I put my toys away.
when	We stop when the bell rings.
have	We have toys and books at home.
school	We go home after school.
from	I took a book from the shelf
one	Write the word for the number 1.
two	Write the word for the number 2.
jump	I jump in the pool when it is hot.
with	I play with my friends.
frog	A frog makes a croaking sound.
must	You must cross the road carefully.
her	Give the present to her.
play	We play in the playground.
happy	I smile when I am happy.

Mark /15

Ten Point Checklist

The student has demonstrated the ability to ...

○ confidently relate letter names to their sounds to read and spell simple text.

○ differentiate between long and short sounds in word families and core words.

○ understand and apply both long and short sounds when deciphering and writing simple text.

○ recognise word families where words rhyme and have a common base

○ slide sounds together to make common blends such as pl, st, dr, etc.

○ recognise and apply special blends - th, sh, wh, ch in word families and core words.

○ build on word families to extend beyond the examples given

○ recognise sight words and use phonic clues to help decipher them

○ build their own personal word bank

○ read simple compound words and create some of their own using known words in word families.

○ use the knowledge and word attack skills learnt through oral and written activities to read and spell new words.

○ construct one or more readable sentences.